Alan

Happy Christmas 2014

love Jenny x

WILLIAM MORRIS

A SENSE OF PLACE

WILLIAM MORRIS
A SENSE OF PLACE
26 JUNE - 17 OCTOBER 2010

FOREWORD

Blackwell has a 'sense of place' like few other houses, and is the ideal venue for an exhibition exploring how William Morris's work was influenced by this elusive quality. Blackwell's curator, Dr Kathy Haslam, has brought together a wealth of designs, books, images and textiles to illustrate how Morris's feel for place shaped his life's work and philosophy. Blackwell itself is a reminder of the legacy he left as the 'Father' of the Arts & Crafts Movement, redolent of the qualities he promoted.

We have been fortunate to have the support of many collectors and institutions, most importantly the William Morris Society, in association with which the exhibition has been developed. We are also grateful to the Golsoncott Foundation for supporting the exhibition, as well as to all our lenders. In her essay for this publication Dr Haslam explores the theme of a 'sense of place' with reference to works in the show; it is followed by a vivid essay by the renowned Morris scholar Peter Faulkner.

The final few pages of this catalogue form a William Morris 'trail' around the North of England, taking in collections and venues with a link to Morris and which are open to the public. They reveal the extent of Morris' legacy as a thinker and designer, as well as the 'progress' he challenged, and remind us of his influence in this region. We are grateful to the Industrial Powerhouse group of venues for assistance with this section.

Adam Naylor
Chairman of the Trustees
Lakeland Arts Trust

'THE WORLD GOES ON, BEAUTIFUL AND STRANGE AND DREADFUL AND WORSHIPFUL'

ABOVE:
WILLIAM MORRIS AS A YOUNG MAN
c.1850
PHOTOGRAPH
© WILLIAM MORRIS GALLERY, LONDON
BOROUGH OF WALTHAM FOREST

OPPOSITE:
VIEW OF THE RIVER AT KELMSCOTT
1897
FREDERICK H EVANS
PHOTOGRAPH
© THE ESTATE OF FREDERICK H EVANS

This exhibition looks at William Morris from a fresh perspective: his sense of place – within the domestic sphere, in his design work and writings, his conservation work, and in his feelings about the wider environment of countryside and city in an aggressively industrialised age. The instinctive sense of 'rightness' he felt about place is a recurring theme in contemporary accounts of Morris and was an underlying factor in his wellbeing, creativity and the development of his ideas on a fairer society which reached their logical conclusion in 1883 when he committed himself to Socialism.

William Morris (1834-96) was born into an affluent middle-class family and grew up in what he later described as "the ordinary bourgeois style of comfort." His early homes were key to forming his precocious sense of place and the love of nature that underpinned his subsequent life and thinking. At Woodford Hall in Essex, where the family lived between 1840 and 1848, the young Morris had his own garden and studied the plants and flowers in John Gerard's *Herball* (first published in 1597), early evidence of his voracious appetite for practical knowledge. Woodford Hall's fifty-acre park adjoined Epping Forest, and Morris grew to appreciate its special character, calling it "always interesting and always beautiful". Epping Forest was ancient woodland, and its appeal to Morris lay in its claims as a fragmentary survival of past ages, as well as in its natural beauty; later in life he campaigned against plans to fell parts of the Forest for development.

8

OPPOSITE:
DESIGNS FOR THE DECORATION OF RED
HOUSE
THE WEDDING FEAST OF SIR DEGREVAUNT
EDWARD BURNE-JONES
1860
WATERCOLOUR AND GOUACHE
© FITZWILLIAM MUSEUM, CAMBRIDGE

The family move to Water House, Walthamstow, came in 1848 and for several years it was here that Morris came home for the school holidays. He loved the moat in the grounds, manifesting the pleasure that he was to take for the rest of his life in water and rivers, which would become so much a part of his designs and writings. He protested on more than one occasion against the threat to rivers posed by industrial development and came to regard the Thames with almost proprietorial affection, going on to make a series of designs named after the Thames and its tributaries. His last London home, Kelmscott House, stood next to the Thames just below Hammersmith Bridge, and his rented country home, Kelmscott Manor, was also within sight of the river; Morris would return repeatedly to rivers in his writings and in his own life as places of escape, beauty and continuity.

Morris formed the cornerstone relationships of his life whilst at Exeter College, Oxford (1853-1855), where he met fellow undergraduates Edward Burne-Jones, Charles Faulkner and the group of young men who would become the Oxford Brotherhood. Morris and Burne-Jones, who had both planned to be ordained into the Church after leaving university, instead decided to embark on "a life of art" – Burne-Jones as an artist and Morris as an architect. In 1856 Morris entered the office of the Oxford-based Gothic revival architect George Edmund Street. Whilst training in Street's office he met and formed a close and lifelong friendship with Philip Webb, who later described the young Morris as "a slim boy like a wonderful bird just out of his shell." He planned to combine his architectural training with studying life drawing, having been encouraged to take up painting by the artist Dante Gabriel Rossetti, a charismatic and influential figure in Morris's early development. The following year, 1857, Morris met and fell in love with Jane Burden, the daughter of an Oxford stableman, who modelled for his painting *La Belle Iseult*. They were married two years later.

It was to Philip Webb that Morris turned in 1859 for the design of his first married home, Red House in Bexleyheath,

LEFT:
CARTOON FOR *ARTEMIS*
c.1860
DESIGNED BY WILLIAM MORRIS AS ONE OF
A SEQUENCE OF EMBROIDERED PANELS
FOR RED HOUSE
INK, CHALK AND WASH
© TULLIE HOUSE MUSEUM & ART GALLERY

OPPOSITE TOP:
TILE, *DAISY*
1860s
DESIGNED BY WILLIAM MORRIS FOR
MORRIS, MARSHALL, FAULKNER & CO.
EARTHENWARE
© WILLIAM MORRIS GALLERY, LONDON
BOROUGH OF WALTHAM FOREST

OPPOSITE MIDDLE:
TILE, *COCKEREL*
1860s
DESIGNED BY PHILIP WEBB FOR MORRIS,
MARSHALL, FAULKNER & CO.
EARTHENWARE
© WILLIAM MORRIS GALLERY, LONDON
BOROUGH OF WALTHAM FOREST

OPPOSITE BOTTOM:
TILE, *DUCK*
1860s
DESIGNED BY PHILIP WEBB FOR MORRIS,
MARSHALL, FAULKNER & CO.
EARTHENWARE
© WILLIAM MORRIS GALLERY, LONDON
BOROUGH OF WALTHAM FOREST

then a semi-rural setting. Morris planned to make it "the beautifullest place on earth". Between 1856 and 1859 Morris had lived with Burne-Jones in three-room lodgings at 17 Red Lion Square in London. When Morris and Burne-Jones took them, the lodgings were unfurnished. Having failed to locate furniture with which he could feel at home, and recognising that the character and ambience of his domestic environment was fundamental to him, Morris had designed several pieces himself. These were large, solid items and the table was, according to the artist DG Rossetti "as firm, and as heavy, as a rock". Morris and Burne-Jones, with some involvement from Rossetti and Charles Faulkner, decorated them with "knights and ladies" and subjects taken from Morris's early poetry such as Sir Galahad and Rapunzel. The lodgings at Red Lion Square thus acquired something of a Medieval feel; in Burne-Jones's words "Topsy [Morris] and I live together in the quaintest room in all London, hung with brasses of old knights and drawings of Albert Durer." Morris was to become renowned for his energy, and the Red Lion Square period became a time for him to explore crafts that had their origins in the Medieval period, such as wood-carving and illuminating manuscripts, whilst also continuing his training in drawing and painting.

In tune with his taste, the house that Webb designed for him was described by Morris as "very medieval in spirit"; Red House was dubbed 'the Towers of Topsy' by Rossetti. The newlyweds moved in during June 1860. In his lecture *How We Live and How We Might Live* (1884) Morris described what the concept of 'home' represented to him: "...my home is where I meet people with whom I sympathise, whom I love"; his description was epitomised by the Red House days, which had at their heart this ideal combination of friendship and collaboration. The house became the focus of creativity for Morris and his friends in the early years of his marriage; painting and embroidery went hand-in-hand with games of hide-and-seek and practical jokes. Georgiana Burne-Jones remembered the tenor of these days: "here they laid plans for the future, discussed work going on at the moment, and in the intervals told anecdotes and played

SED ·POETA TURPITER
SITIENS CANESCIT

TO
J.M.
from
EBJ.

the above will be home
2 tonight—

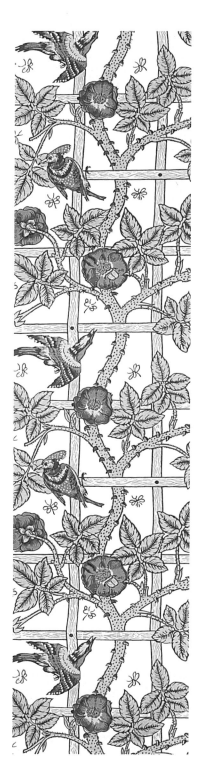

each other tricks which prolonged the youth that seemed as if it would never fail." This experience of working together to create an interior of beauty and originality was to give rise to the ambitious idea of founding a furnishing company.

During the process of developing the interiors at Red House, Morris had found that his true *métier* lay in design, and in January 1861 Burne-Jones announced that "he and Morris and Rossetti and Webb were going to set up a sort of shop where they would jointly produce and sell furniture." There were in fact seven partners, the other three being Charles Faulkner, Peter Paul Marshall and the painter Ford Madox Brown. The Firm, as it was fondly known, had premises at 8 Red Lion Square between 1861 and 1865; in that year new premises at 26 Queen Square were leased, and Morris and his family lived 'above the shop' there until 1872. Queen Square remained the Firm's premises until 1881.

To showcase its products the Firm stood at the 1862 International Exhibition; it described itself in its prospectus as "Fine Workmen in Painting, Carving, Furniture and the Metals", stating that it would undertake carving, stained glass, metal-work, paper-hangings, chintzes (printed fabrics), and carpets. Commissions for stained glass proved an important element of the Firm's early work.

The Firm's partners worked closely together in responding to commissions. Their approach laid the foundation for what would become the Arts & Crafts Movement. The current exhibition examines one notable commission, for the decoration of 1 Palace Green in Kensington, a house designed in 1867 by Webb for George Howard (1843-1911), a young man who was both artist and aristocrat. Howard had studied painting briefly with Burne-Jones, resulting in a close and lengthy friendship. In her reminiscences of her husband, Georgiana Burne-Jones later acknowledged that Howard and his wife Rosalind were numbered amongst the very few people to be admitted into the "magic circle" of friends that formed their close-knit group.

MR MORRIS reading poems to MR BURNE JONES

The Palace Green building plot was owned by the Crown, and Webb's design proved controversial, attracting seemingly endless objections from the Office of Woods and Forests, which managed the Crown Estates; it was not actually completed until 1872. The decoration of Palace Green was a collaborative project in which Webb, Burne-Jones and Morris all had a hand, and its crowning glory was the dining room, with its dramatic *Cupid and Psyche* frieze, designed by Burne-Jones. The decoration of the ceiling and the painted and gilded decoration of the woodwork surrounding the frieze panels was undertaken by Morris, the result being a room that glowed "like the page of an illuminated missal." Palace Green was an influential house, both in its design and decoration, and many years later was still being appraised as such: "It would seem a rash statement to affirm of the decoration of any single apartment that it was absolutely the best example of the style it obeyed. Yet if ever it were safe to speak thus unreservedly, it might be concerning the beautiful dining room at...Palace Green, representing as it does the united efforts of Burne-Jones, William Morris and Philip Webb." (*Studio* magazine, 1899)

The boudoir at Palace Green was to be decorated as a backdrop for Burne-Jones's painting *The Annunciation*, and it is evident from surviving correspondence that Morris was inexhaustible in his commitment to creating a harmonious interior. He and Burne-Jones trekked to the house several times with fabrics and wallpaper samples before they were satisfied that the best patterns and colours had been selected. Morris wrote to Howard: "Ned [Burne-Jones] and I went to Palace Green yesterday and our joint conclusion was that the best hanging for the walls of the boudoir would be the enclosed madder-printed cotton: it brings out the greys of the picture better than anything else. Also I think it would make a pretty room with the woodwork painted a light blue-green colour like a starling's egg..."

In 1871 Morris began looking for "a little house out of London" where he could find relief from city life from time to time. On discovering Kelmscott Manor in a remote setting near

WILLIAM MORRIS'S BEDROOM AT
KELMSCOTT MANOR
c.1915
MARY SLOANE
WATERCOLOUR
© WILLIAM MORRIS GALLERY, LONDON
BOROUGH OF WALTHAM FOREST

Lechlade in the Cotswolds he wrote to Charley Faulkner, that it was "a heaven on earth; an old stone Elizabethan house... and such a garden! Close down on the river, a boat house and all things handy." Traces of the original garden even survived. Morris loved the house, its oneness with the countryside that formed its setting, and the hundreds of years during which it had mellowed until it had become, in his eyes, a place of special beauty. It became his "harbour of refuge". Looking at Kelmscott Manor's roof tiles, Morris wrote, "gives one the same sort of pleasure in their orderly beauty as a fish's scale or a bird's feather". The depth of his feeling for the house is expressed in his words: "As others love the race of man through their lovers and children, so I love the earth through that small space of it".

In Morris's utopian novel *News from Nowhere*, published in 1890, Kelmscott Manor featured as "the old house by the Thames". In *News from Nowhere* Morris conveyed the sense of belonging and comfort to be found in this ancient place and in the continuity of a largely unchanged and unspoilt rural community. Morris initially took Kelmscott Manor on a joint tenancy with Rossetti for an annual rent of £75, and after Rossetti gave up his claims to it in 1874 Morris renewed the tenancy jointly with his friend and publisher FS Ellis, continuing to rent the property until his death in 1896.

There could not be a stronger contrast to Kelmscott than Iceland, another place at the forefront of Morris's mind during the early 1870s. He had recently taught himself Icelandic and set about translating the Icelandic sagas with scholar Eiríkr Magnússon. Morris visited Iceland for two memorable trips in 1871 and 1873, developing a deep affection for the wild barren grandeur of its scenery and the simplicity and resilience of its people. The impressions left by them remained with him throughout his life, often resurfacing; for example, he was to write in 1874 from George Howard's ancestral home Naworth Castle in Cumbria: "We had a long drive yesterday...and I sniffed the smell of the moors and felt in Iceland again."

18

With the Firm having expanded and outgrown the Queen Square premises, in 1881 Morris set about searching for a new site suitable for production on a larger scale. After much looking he located Merton Abbey, a former silk-weaving factory in south-west London. Morris's criteria combined the practical and romantic; he was unable to work in an environment that gave him no pleasure, and the Merton Abbey site – a rambling building with weather-boarded sheds standing beside the tree-lined River Wandle and a mill pond bright with marsh marigolds – felt 'right' to him. With his instinct for place, he declared that Merton would "fit us like an old shoe". As his daughter May was later to comment: "one can scarcely imagine him settled in a neat brick factory...among utilitarian buildings of unengaging aspect."

Merton Abbey was the site for the Firm's production of printed textiles, tapestries, carpets, and stained glass but even amidst this noisy working environment Nature and domesticity were always close at hand; later, May Morris remembered "the dye-shop with...white steam curling about the roof, the sunlight outside and the willow boughs pressed close against the windows." Morris created a flower garden and vegetable garden on the site, with plots for some of the workmen. Thomas Wardle, the Firm's manager, recalled that "There seems nothing to say except that it was altogether delightful."

Morris harboured a vision for the infusion of inspiration, through art and nature, into the everyday lives of ordinary people. The industrial society into which Britain had evolved represented inequality, exploitation and ugliness to him, setting him on the path to Socialism and the foundation of the Society for the Protection of Ancient Buildings. He referred to London as a "spreading sore...mocking our feeble efforts to deal even with its minor evils of smoke-laden sky and befouled river". In 1883 Morris crossed "the river of fire" and became an actively-campaigning revolutionary Socialist, although it is clear that his political views and frustration with British society as it had evolved had been taking shape over many years. In 1874 he

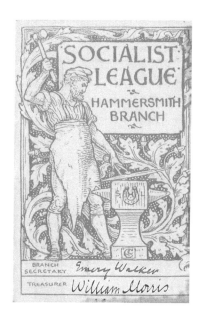

had written: "...suppose people lived in little communities among gardens and green fields...and had few wants; almost no furniture for instance, and no servants, and studied the difficult arts of enjoying life, and finding out what they really wanted: then I think one might hope civilization had really begun." This plea for a simpler, fairer society uncompromised by the greed and self-interest of a capitalist system was repeated in seemingly inexhaustible permutations in his subsequent writings, speeches and lectures. *News from Nowhere*, for example, presents a post-revolution England, a society in which the evils of commerce have been swept away both physically and ideologically. The great industrial cities such as Manchester exist no more, and London is changed beyond recognition: 'The soap-works with their smoke-vomiting chimneys were gone; the engineer's works gone; the lead-works gone; and no sound of rivetting and hammering came down the west wind from Thorneycroft's.' Morris, in the guise of narrator, feels free from 'that dread of approaching ruin, which had always beset me ...when I had been amongst the beautiful works of art of the past, mingled with the lovely nature of the present.'

Morris's unwillingness to stand by as a passive witness to the ruination of a land which he loved so deeply underpinned his commitment to the Socialist cause. It was to prove an exhausting commitment.

Morris was not naturally suited to public life or public speaking but his belief that "To complain and not to act, that is to waste one's life", spurred him on to involvement with many different organizations as well as the Socialist and Movement. In 1877 he became honorary secretary for the Society for the Protection of Ancient Buildings (SPAB), which he co-founded to counteract the aggressive restoration of historical buildings. For its first public circular Morris composed a message that summed up his belief that we are merely custodians of what history has bequeathed us, and which has formed our identity as a nation: "Take proper care of your monuments...Watch an old building with an anxious care; count its stones as you would the jewels of a crown; bind it together with iron where it loosens, stay it

THIS IS THE PICTURE OF THE OLD HOUSE BY THE THAMES TO WHICH THE PEOPLE OF THIS STORY WENT. HEREAFTER FOLLOWS THE BOOK ITSELF WHICH IS CALLED NEWS FROM NOWHERE OR AN EPOCH OF REST & IS WRITTEN BY WILLIAM MORRIS.

NEWS FROM NOWHERE OR AN EPOCH OF REST. CHAPTER I. DISCUSSION AND BED.

UP at the League, says a friend, there had been one night a brisk conversational discussion, as to what would happen on the Morrow of the Revolution, finally shading off into a vigorous statement by various friends, of their views on the future of the fully developed new society.

SAYS our friend: Considering the subject, the discussion was good-tempered; for those present, being used to public meetings & after-lecture debates, if they did not listen to each other's opinions, which could scarcely be expected of them, at all events did not always attempt to speak all together, as is the custom of people in ordinary polite society when conversing

When Adam delved and Eve span
Who was then the gentleman

with timber where it declines...and do this tenderly, reverently, continually, and many a generation will still be born to pass away beneath its shadow." SPAB still exists today, continuing the work that Morris started.

There was for Morris a sense of being condemned to live in a place and time already too compromised by the stamp of industrialisation and the social inequalities that went with it. In his writings, many of which were printed as part of his final great endeavour, the Kelmscott Press, Morris created entire Utopian countries and societies, places of otherness governed by different laws and with different values from the civilization he had grown to despise.

William Morris died aged sixty-two; he was said to have died simply from *being* William Morris. He had exhausted himself in creating, observing, preserving and campaigning for what was a dearly held but simple vision and he remains as relevant to us today as he was when he wrote these prophetic words expressing powerlessness and pathos in his description of the ever-expanding city and the commerce upon which it fed:
"Is there money to be made? Cut down the pleasant trees among the houses, pull down ancient and venerable buildings for the money that a few square yards of London dirt will fetch; blacken rivers, hide the sun and poison the air with smoke and worse, and it's nobody's business to see to it or mend it: that is all that modern commerce, the counting-house forgetful of the workshop, will do for us."

Dr Kathy Haslam
Curator
Blackwell, The Arts & Crafts House

'A SIGH OF PLEASED SURPRISE' MORRIS'S RESPONSE TO LANDSCAPE

As this exhibition clearly shows, William Morris responded with remarkable sensitivity to the various places in which he spent his busy life, and in particular celebrated those in which the beauty and power of nature were most distinctly revealed. In this he was part of the wider Romantic movement that drew attention to the natural environment, at a time when the 'dark Satanic mills' of industrial capitalism were changing the face of Britain for ever. From Wordsworth in the Lake District through Emily Brontë on the Yorkshire moors, Hardy in Wessex and Richard Jefferies in Wiltshire, to Henry Williamson in Devon and the environmentally concerned writers of our own time, the tradition has become a powerful one, and Morris contributed substantially to it. From his days as a schoolboy at Marlborough wandering the downs and finding the ancient stones of Avebury, to the end of his comparatively short life, Morris's writings show the depth of his responses. But what was remarkable about Morris was the way he related the scenery he enjoyed to the society of which it was part. In the poem 'June', for example, published in the second volume of his long poem *The Earthly Paradise* in 1868, we encounter a beautiful landscape evocatively described:

> *Across the river thy soft breezes blow*
> *Sweet with the scent of beanfields far away,*
> *Above our heads rustle the aspens grey,*
> *Calm is the sky with harmless clouds beset,*
> *No thought of storm the morning vexes yet.*

But, as the final line suggests, vexation may be in the offing, and the next stanza shows its source:

See, we have left our hopes and fears behind
To give our very hearts up unto thee;
What better place than this then could we find
By this sweet stream that knows not of the sea,
That guesses not the city's misery,
This little stream whose hamlets scarce have names,
This far-off, lonely mother of the Thames?

However beautiful the scene evoked here in the remote countryside, 'the city's misery', which represents the new and exploitative Britain, cannot be forgotten, and never is by Morris.

In the lecture he gave in 1877 now known as 'The Lesser Arts', Morris expressed his deep feeling for the English countryside, which to some extent retained the qualities of communality that industrialism was destroying; but it is notable the countryside he is describing is a fully inhabited one, and that he is as concerned with the dwellings man has made for himself as with the scenery. He asks his audience to make a journey with him:

...when we can get beyond the smoky world, there, out
in the country we may still see the works of your fathers
yet alive amidst the very nature they were wrought into,
and of which they are so completely a part; for there
indeed if anywhere, in the English countryside, in the
days when people cared about such things, was there
full sympathy between the works of man and the land
they were made for...

He brings out for his listeners what was for him the most appealing aspect of this countryside, its suitability for human habitation: there are no great wastes overwhelming in their dreariness, no great solitudes of forests, no terrible untrodden mountain-walls; all is measured, mingled, varied, gliding easily one thing into another: little rivers, little plains, swelling, speedily-changing uplands, all beset with handsome orderly trees: little hills, little mountains, netted over with the walls of sheep-walks: all is little; yet not foolish and blank, but serious rather, and abundant of meaning for such as choose to seek it: it is neither prison nor palace, but a decent home.

It is clear that this kind of domesticated English landscape had a profound appeal to Morris, who was particularly attached to the notion of 'home'. But he could write equally evocatively of the very different landscape of Iceland, which he visited in 1871 and 1873, drawn there largely by his feeling for the courage of the people as shown in the sagas, which he had recently started to translate with the help of his Icelandic friend, Eirikr Magnusson. The opening of his poem 'Iceland First Seen' (published later in *Poems by the Way* in 1891) gives a vigorous account of his reaction to the sight of this 'desolate strand' as he approached it for the first time:

> Lo from our loitering ship a new land at last to be seen;
> Toothed rocks down the side of the firth on the east
> guard a weary wide lea,
> And black slope the hillsides above, striped adown
> with their desolate green:
> And a peak rises up on the west from the meeting of
> cloud and of sea,
> Foursquare from base unto point like the building of
> Gods that have been,
> The last of that waste of the mountains all cloud-
> wreathed and snow-flecked and grey,
> And bright with the dawn that began just now at the
> ending of day.

Morris also wrote powerfully in prose about the extraordinary landscape. He kept journals on these visits for his friend Georgiana Burne-Jones; they were not intended for publication, though they were published after his death. In his entry for Saturday 29th July 1871 Morris recorded in powerful detail his journey 'From the Geysirs through the Wilderness to Vatnsdalur':

> Meanwhile we have put Hlodufell behind us, but Skjaldbreidur is still unchanged on our left: on our right is a mass of jagged bare mountains, all beset with clouds, that, drifting away now and then show dreadful inaccessible ravines and closed up valleys with no trace of grass about them among the toothed peaks and rent walls; I think it is the most horrible sight of mountains I had the whole journey long.

No wonder that Morris admired the courage of the people he met here, living lives of simplicity and dignity amid such uncomfortably un-English scenes. He was also greatly impressed by the freedom of the Icelanders from the constrictions of the British class system.

Morris was never a tourist; he was far too busy with his design work and later his Socialist undertakings to spend his time in this way. Thus he did not follow the developing fashion of his times for visiting the Lake District. When he did come north it was usually to visit his and Jane's friends, George and Rosalind Howard, at Naworth Castle near Carlisle. But Morris's most positive remark about the north occurred in a letter to his daughter Jenny of 28th April 1885, when he had travelled on the railway from Carlisle to Settle on his way to visit Edward Carpenter, who had recently set himself up as market gardener near Sheffield:

> *...though I knew it was a beautiful journey... I was really quite surprised at the beauty of the country; I think it is the loveliest part of all England: I will tell you about it when I see you. If ever we 'retire from active service' I must sit down somewhere near Kirkby Stephen.*

He then adds, characteristically and no doubt accurately: "The manufacturing districts (from Skipton onwards) looked awful after this..." As we know, Morris never did 'retire from active service'.

However, it must be remembered that Morris was an imaginative writer, in both verse and prose, just as capable of creating in convincing detail places that never existed as evoking those that did. The early 'Story of the Unknown Church' (first published in the Oxford and Cambridge Magazine in 1856) shows how accomplished Morris was in this mode while still an undergraduate. The description is of a building and its setting in the early Middle Ages; the narrator is the church-builder, and he describes the abbey near where the church was built as surrounded by a circle of poplars. The effect of the breeze on these trees is described in beautiful detail:

> *...and whenever a wind passed over them, were it ever so little a breath, it set them all a-ripple; and when the wind was high, they bowed and swayed very low, and the wind, as it lifted the leaves, and showed their silvery white sides, or as again in the lulls of it, it let them drop, kept on changing the trees from green to white, and from white to green...*

We are then shown the view beyond:

> *...moreover, through the boughs and trunks of the poplars we caught glimpses of the great golden corn sea, waving, waving, waving for leagues and leagues; and among the corn grew burning scarlet poppies and blue corn-flowers; and the corn-flowers were so blue, that they gleamed, and seemed to burn with a steady light, as they grew beside the poppies among the gold of the wheat. Through the corn sea ran a blue river, & always green meadows and lines of tall poplars followed its windings.*

The poplars may suggest a French setting, but the emphasis on the flowers brings us closer to the fabric and wallpaper designs which were soon to flow from Morris's pen rather than to any specific landscape. Morris continued to create memorable imaginative settings for the events of his much later Prose Romances, as they are usually called, such as *The Wood Beyond the World* of 1894, *The Water of the Wondrous Isles* of 1895, *The Well at the World's End* of 1896, and the posthumously published *Sundering Flood* of 1897.

However, it will be fitting to conclude with *News from Nowhere*, published in book form in 1891, in which Morris gave his finest account of the country that he would like England to become, a thriving co-operative community based on fellowship and concern for the environment. The novel effectively contrasts, not town and country, but town and country as they were in Morris's time, soiled by commerce and its exploitation of people and the land, and town and country after the revolution. Near the end of the story, the narrator, William Guest, is taken by his young guide Ellen to an old house on the Thames, where the scene is described with deep affection:

> My companion gave a sigh of pleased surprise and enjoyment; nor did I wonder, for the garden between the wall and the house was redolent of the June flowers, and the roses were rolling over one another with that delicious super-abundance of small well-tended gardens which at first sight takes away all thought from the beholder save that of beauty. The blackbirds were singing their loudest, the doves were cooing on the roof-ridge, the rooks in the high elm-trees beyond were garrulous among the young leaves, and the swifts wheeled whining about the gables. And the house itself was a fit guardian for all the beauty of this heart of summer.

Here Morris brings to life a scene very dear to his heart, based on his experience of living for periods at Kelmscott Manor, on the Oxfordshire/Gloucestershire border, which he rented from 1873 to the end of his life; his tomb, designed by his friend Philip Webb, is in Kelmscott churchyard.

The scene described is indeed beautiful; but it must be emphasised that its perfection is presented to the reader as part of the society created by the revolution, which values human creativity over the profit motive and so preserves the best of the past while creating its new world of community and peace. *News from Nowhere* thus reminds us that beautiful landscapes are seldom accidental but are usually created by human activity. When we respond to Morris's sense of place, it should be not only by appreciating in aesthetic terms the scenes that he describes. We should follow his example by also responding politically, by participating in organisations that exist to further the aims that *News from Nowhere* so attractively conveys, and by aligning ourselves with whatever political party we feel is most strongly committed to the environmentalist cause.

SOURCES
AND SUGGESTIONS
FOR FURTHER
READING

Peter Faulkner, editor, *William Morris. Selected Poems.*
Carcanet Press 1992 (contains the poems quoted).

Norman Kelvin, editor, *The Collected Letters of William Morris.*
4 volumes, Princeton University Press 1984-1996.

Fiona MacCarthy, *William Morris. A Life for Our Time.*
Faber and Faber, 1994.

Magnus Magnusson, editor, *William Morris. The Icelandic
Journals.* Mare's Nest 1996.

E.P.Thompson, *William Morris. Romantic to Revolutionary.*
1955; revised edition, Merlin press, 1977.

Paul Thompson, *The Work of William Morris.*
Oxford University Press 1967.

Clive Wilmer, editor, *William Morris. News from Nowhere and
Other Writings.*
Penguin 1993 (also contains 'The Lesser Arts').

Peter Faulkner
Emeritus, Honorary University Fellow
The University of Exeter

LIST OF WORKS

TILE PANEL, *POPPY*
1870s
DESIGNED BY WILLIAM MORRIS
FOR MORRIS & CO
EARTHENWARE
BIRKENHEAD COLLECTION
ILLUSTRATED ON PAGE 37

TILE PANEL, *FOLIAGE*
c.1870-75
DESIGNED BY WILLIAM MORRIS
FOR MORRIS & CO
EARTHENWARE
BIRKENHEAD COLLECTION

TILE, *SWAN*
c.1903
DESIGNED c.1863 BY WILLIAM
MORRIS FOR MORRIS,
MARSHALL, FAULKNER & CO
EARTHENWARE
BIRKENHEAD COLLECTION

SCREEN PANEL, *APPLE TREE*
1890s
DESIGNED BY JH DEARLE FOR
MORRIS & CO
WOOD, SILK
BIRKENHEAD COLLECTION
ILLUSTRATED ON PAGE 33 (DETAIL)

SCREEN PANEL,
POMEGRANATE TREE
1890s
DESIGNED BY JH DEARLE FOR
MORRIS & CO
WOOD, SILK
BIRKENHEAD COLLECTION

TILE, *COLUMBINE*
1860s
DESIGNED BY WILLIAM MORRIS
FOR MORRIS, MARSHALL,
FAULKNER & CO
EARTHENWARE
BIRKENHEAD COLLECTION
ILLUSTRATED ON PAGE 41

TILE PANEL, *MINSTREL WITH
HARP*
LATE 19TH CENTURY
ORIGINALLY DESIGNED BY
WILLIAM MORRIS FOR MORRIS,
MARSHALL, FAULKNER & CO
EARTHENWARE
BIRKENHEAD COLLECTION

TILE PANEL, *MINSTREL WITH
DOUBLE PIPES*
LATE 19TH CENTURY
ORIGINALLY DESIGNED IN
1867 BY WILLIAM MORRIS FOR
MORRIS, MARSHALL, FAULKNER
& CO
EARTHENWARE
BIRKENHEAD COLLECTION
ILLUSTRATED ON PAGE 33

STAINED GLASS PANEL, *MAGPIE*
c.1860
DESIGNED BY PHILIP WEBB
AND PROBABLY PRODUCED
BY JAMES POWELL & SONS,
WHITEFRIARS
GLASS
BIRKENHEAD COLLECTION
ILLUSTRATED ON PAGE 41

DESIGN FOR A TILE PANEL,
THE ORGAN PLAYER
1867-8
DESIGNED BY WILLIAM MORRIS
FOR MORRIS, MARSHALL,
FAULKNER & CO
PENCIL, INK, SEPIA
WHITWORTH ART GALLERY, THE
UNIVERSITY OF MANCHESTER

DESIGN FOR *WILLOW BOUGHS*
WALLPAPER
1887
DESIGNED BY WILLIAM MORRIS
FOR MORRIS & CO
PENCIL, WATERCOLOUR
WHITWORTH ART GALLERY, THE
UNIVERSITY OF MANCHESTER

SAMPLES OF MADDER DYED
INDIAN SILK
WHITWORTH ART GALLERY, THE
UNIVERSITY OF MANCHESTER

HAMMERSMITH WALLPAPER
SAMPLE
DESIGNED IN 1890 BY WILLIAM
MORRIS FOR MORRIS & CO
BLOCK-PRINTED PAPER
WHITWORTH ART GALLERY, THE
UNIVERSITY OF MANCHESTER

TRELLIS WALLPAPER SAMPLE
DESIGNED IN 1864 BY WILLIAM
MORRIS AND PHILIP WEBB FOR
MORRIS & CO
BLOCK-PRINTED PAPER
WHITWORTH ART GALLERY, THE
UNIVERSITY OF MANCHESTER

PAGE 312 FROM 'THE
CANTERBURY TALES' IN THE
WORKS OF GEOFFREY CHAUCER
1896
HAMMERSMITH: KELMSCOTT
PRESS
PAPER
WHITWORTH ART GALLERY, THE
UNIVERSITY OF MANCHESTER

ALBUM CONTAINING 38
WOODCUTS OF *CUPID & PSYCHE*
c.1880
COMPILED AND TITLED BY
WILLIAM MORRIS
WHITWORTH ART GALLERY, THE
UNIVERSITY OF MANCHESTER

HEADPIECE TO THE PROLOGUE
OF *'THE CANTERBURY TALES'*
IN THE *WORKS OF GEOFFREY
CHAUCER*
1896
HAMMERSMITH: KELMSCOTT
PRESS
PAPER
WHITWORTH ART GALLERY, THE
UNIVERSITY OF MANCHESTER

*STUDY FOR THE WEDDING FEAST
OF SIR DEGREVAUNT*
1860
DESIGNED BY EDWARD
BURNE-JONES FOR A WALL
PAINTING AT RED HOUSE
WATERCOLOUR, AND
GOUACHE ON PAPER
FITZWILLIAM MUSEUM,
CAMBRIDGE

*WILLIAM MORRIS, WORKING ON A
TAPESTRY, VIEWED FROM BEHIND*
1880s
EDWARD BURNE-JONES
GRAPHITE ON PAPER
FITZWILLIAM MUSEUM,
CAMBRIDGE

PRINTING BLOCK, '*PSYCHE IS
SET THE TASK OF COLLECTING
THE GOLDEN FLEECE FROM
VENUS' FLOCKS AND IS HELPED
BY A VOICE FROM THE REEDS'*
FOR *THE STORY OF CUPID &
PSYCHE*
1880
WOOD, CUT BY WILLIAM MORRIS
SOCIETY OF ANTIQUARIES OF
LONDON

PRINTING BLOCK, *'THE KING AND THE HANDMAIDENS ACCOMPANYING PSYCHE TO THE MOUNTAIN'* FOR *THE STORY OF CUPID & PSYCHE*
1880
WOOD, CUT BY WILLIAM MORRIS
SOCIETY OF ANTIQUARIES OF LONDON

PRINTING BLOCK, *'PSYCHE'S DESCENT INTO HADES'* FOR THE STORY OF *CUPID & PSYCHE*
1880
WOOD, CUT BY WILLIAM MORRIS
SOCIETY OF ANTIQUARIES OF LONDON

BOOK-BINDING TOOLS
KELMSCOTT PRESS (FOR KELMSCOTT CHAUCER)
WOOD, STEEL, BRASS
SOCIETY OF ANTIQUARIES OF LONDON

SED POETA TURPITER SITIENS CANESCIT
1865-80
EDWARD BURNE-JONES
PENCIL AND INK ON PAPER
THE TRUSTEES OF THE BRITISH MUSEUM

ROSSETTI AND HIS CIRCLE
1922
MAX BEERBOHM
HEINEMANN, LONDON
LAKELAND ARTS TRUST
ILLUSTRATED ON PAGE 38

TILE, *COCKEREL*
1860s
DESIGNED BY PHILIP WEBB FOR MORRIS, MARSHALL, FAULKNER & CO.
EARTHENWARE
WILLIAM MORRIS GALLERY, LONDON BOROUGH OF WALTHAM FOREST

TILE, *DUCK*
1860s
DESIGNED BY PHILIP WEBB FOR MORRIS, MARSHALL, FAULKNER & CO.
EARTHENWARE
WILLIAM MORRIS GALLERY, LONDON BOROUGH OF WALTHAM FOREST

TILE, *DAISY*
EARLY 1860s
DESIGNED BY WILLIAM MORRIS FOR MORRIS, MARSHALL, FAULKNER & CO.
EARTHENWARE
WILLIAM MORRIS GALLERY, LONDON BOROUGH OF WALTHAM FOREST

MORRIS FISHING IN A PUNT
1871
DANTE GABRIEL ROSSETTI
PENCIL AND INK ON PAPER
THE TRUSTEES OF THE BRITISH MUSEUM

MR MORRIS READING POEMS TO MR BURNE-JONES
1865-80
EDWARD BURNE-JONES
PENCIL AND INK ON PAPER
THE TRUSTEES OF THE BRITISH MUSEUM

SAMPLES OF WOOL AND SILK; DYE POT; SPATULAS
WILLIAM MORRIS GALLERY, LONDON BOROUGH OF WALTHAM FOREST

VIEW OF THE RIVER AT KELMSCOTT
1897
FREDERICK EVANS
PHOTOGRAPH
WILLIAM MORRIS GALLERY, LONDON BOROUGH OF WALTHAM FOREST

CHURCH AT KELMSCOTT
1897
FREDERICK EVANS
PHOTOGRAPH
WILLIAM MORRIS GALLERY,
LONDON BOROUGH OF
WALTHAM FOREST
ILLUSTRATED ON PAGE 37
© THE ESTATE OF FREDERICK
H EVANS

DRAWING 'WHEN ADAM DELVED
AND EVE SPAN'
1888
EDWARD BURNE-JONES
INK, PENCIL AND CHINESE
WHITE ON PAPER
WILLIAM MORRIS GALLERY,
LONDON BOROUGH OF
WALTHAM FOREST

DESIGN FOR THE TALE OF CUPID
AND PSYCHE – PROCESSION OF
MUSICIANS AND TORCHBEARERS
ACCOMPANYING PSYCHE TO THE
MOUNTAIN
1880
EDWARD BURNE-JONES
WOOD ENGRAVING
BIRMINGHAM MUSEUMS & ART
GALLERY

DESIGN FOR THE TALE OF CUPID
AND PSYCHE – THE KING AND THE
HANDMAIDENS ACCOMPANYING
PSYCHE TO THE MOUNTAIN
1880
EDWARD BURNE-JONES
WOOD ENGRAVING
BIRMINGHAM MUSEUMS & ART
GALLERY

'HAMMERSMITH' RUG
c.1879
DESIGNED BY WILLIAM MORRIS
FOR MORRIS & CO
WOOL, SILK ON A COTTON WARP
WILLIAM MORRIS SOCIETY
ILLUSTRATED ON PAGE 41

CARTOON FOR ARTEMIS
c.1860
INK, RED CHALK AND BROWN
WASH
TULLIE HOUSE MUSEUM & ART
GALLERY

WILLIAM MORRIS'S BEDROOM AT
KELMSCOTT MANOR
c.1915
MARY SLOANE
WATERCOLOUR
WILLIAM MORRIS GALLERY,
LONDON BOROUGH OF
WALTHAM FOREST

MAY MORRIS IN THE TAPESTRY
ROOM AT KELMSCOTT MANOR
c.1915
MARY SLOANE
WATERCOLOUR
WILLIAM MORRIS GALLERY,
LONDON BOROUGH OF
WALTHAM FOREST

POPULAR MUSIC OF THE OLDEN
TIME: A COLLECTION OF ANCIENT
SONGS, BALLADS & DANCE TUNES
ILLUSTRATIVE OF THE NATIONAL
MUSIC OF ENGLAND
c.1858
LONDON: CHAPPELL & CO
LAKELAND ARTS TRUST

THE DEFENCE OF GUENEVERE
AND OTHER POEMS
1858
WILLIAM MORRIS
LONDON: BELL AND DALDY
WILLIAM MORRIS SOCIETY

EMBROIDERY, FEMALE
MINSTREL WITH CYMBALS
1880s
ADAPTED FROM A DESIGN OF
1867 BY WILLIAM MORRIS AND
EXECUTED BY MAY MORRIS
WILLIAM MORRIS SOCIETY
ILLUSTRATED ON PAGE 34

MARIGOLD TEXTILE SAMPLE
DESIGNED IN 1875 BY WILLIAM
MORRIS FOR MORRIS & CO
BLOCK-PRINTED COTTON
TULLIE HOUSE MUSEUM & ART
GALLERY

DESIGN FOR JASMINE
WALLPAPER
1872
DESIGNED BY WILLIAM MORRIS
FOR MORRIS & CO
PENCIL AND WATERCOLOUR
WILLIAM MORRIS SOCIETY
ILLUSTRATED ON PAGE 38

DESIGN FOR BIRD TEXTILE
1878
DESIGNED BY WILLIAM MORRIS
FOR MORRIS & CO
PENCIL AND WATERCOLOUR
WILLIAM MORRIS SOCIETY
SAMPLE ILLUSTRATED ON
PAGE 35 (DETAIL)

LINOLEUM SAMPLE
DESIGNED IN 1875 BY WILLIAM
MORRIS FOR MORRIS & CO
CORTICINE
WILLIAM MORRIS SOCIETY

EMBROIDERY WORK
c.1917
MORRIS & COMPANY
WILLIAM MORRIS SOCIETY

WILLIAM MORRIS
1875
GEORGE HOWARD
PENCIL ON PAPER
TULLIE HOUSE MUSEUM & ART
GALLERY
ILLUSTRATED ON PAGE 39

MORRIS & COMPANY: INTERIOR
DECORATION, FURNITURE,
PANELLING ETC
c.1917
WILLIAM MORRIS SOCIETY

KELMSCOTT MANOR
EARLY 20TH CENTURY
A HALCROW VERSTAGE
HAND-COLOURED LANTERN SLIDE
WILLIAM MORRIS SOCIETY

KELMSCOTT MANOR
EARLY 20TH CENTURY
A HALCROW VERSTAGE
LANTERN SLIDE
WILLIAM MORRIS SOCIETY

SAMPLE OF DAISY WALLPAPER
DESIGNED IN 1864 BY WILLIAM
MORRIS FOR MORRIS,
MARSHALL, FAULKNER & CO
BLOCK-PRINTED PAPER
EMERY WALKER TRUST (02102)

CURTAIN TIE-BACK
TULIP & ROSE
1880s
WOVEN WOOLLEN DOUBLE
CLOTH
EMERY WALKER TRUST

PIMPERNEL WALLPAPER SAMPLE
DESIGNED IN 1876 BY WILLIAM
MORRIS FOR MORRIS & CO
BLOCK-PRINTED PAPER
WILLIAM MORRIS SOCIETY
ILLUSTRATED ON PAGE 39

ADJUSTABLE ARMCHAIR
DESIGNED IN 1861 BY PHILIP
WEBB FOR MORRIS, MARSHALL,
FAULKNER & CO
EBONISED WOOD
PAUL REEVES
ILLUSTRATED ON PAGE 39

'SUSSEX' CHAIR
1870-90
DESIGN ATTRIBUTED TO PHILIP
WEBB c.1860 FOR MORRIS,
MARSHALL, FAULKNER & CO
EBONISED WOOD, RUSH
WILLIAM MORRIS SOCIETY
ILLUSTRATED ON PAGE 34

'SUSSEX' ARMCHAIR
1870-90
DESIGNED BY DANTE GABRIEL
ROSSETTI c.1860 FOR MORRIS,
MARSHALL, FAULKNER & CO
EBONISED WOOD, RUSH
PRIVATE COLLECTION

'SUSSEX' CHAIR
1870-90
DESIGNED c.1860 BY FORD
MADOX BROWN FOR MORRIS,
MARSHALL, FAULKNER & CO
EBONISED WOOD, RUSH
WILLIAM MORRIS SOCIETY

WANDLE TEXTILE SAMPLE
DESIGNED IN 1884 BY WILLIAM
MORRIS FOR MORRIS & CO
BLOCK-PRINTED COTTON
(INDIGO-DISCHARGED)
TULLIE HOUSE MUSEUM & ART
GALLERY

BIRD TEXTILE SAMPLE
DESIGNED IN 1878 BY WILLIAM
MORRIS FOR MORRIS & CO
WOVEN WOOLLEN DOUBLE
CLOTH
WILLIAM MORRIS SOCIETY

JASMINE TRELLIS TEXTILE
SAMPLE
DESIGNED IN 1868-70 BY
WILLIAM MORRIS FOR MORRIS,
MARSHALL, FAULKNER & CO
BLOCK-PRINTED COTTON
TULLIE HOUSE MUSEUM & ART
GALLERY
ILLUSTRATED ON PAGE 35

PRELIMINARY DESIGN FOR
LARKSPUR WALLPAPER
1872
DESIGNED BY WILLIAM MORRIS
FOR MORRIS & CO
PENCIL AND WATERCOLOUR
WILLIAM MORRIS SOCIETY
ILLUSTRATED ON PAGE 43

SNAKESHEAD TEXTILE SAMPLE
DESIGNED IN 1876 BY WILLIAM
MORRIS FOR MORRIS & CO
BLOCK-PRINTED COTTON
TULLIE HOUSE MUSEUM & ART
GALLERY
ILLUSTRATED ON PAGE 42

HONEYSUCKLE TEXTILE SAMPLE
DESIGNED IN 1876 BY WILLIAM
MORRIS FOR MORRIS & CO
BLOCK-PRINTED COTTON
TULLIE HOUSE MUSEUM & ART
GALLERY
ILLUSTRATED ON PAGE 43
(DETAIL)

STRAWBERRY THIEF TEXTILE
SAMPLE
DESIGNED IN 1883 BY WILLIAM
MORRIS FOR MORRIS & CO
BLOCK-PRINTED COTTON
TULLIE HOUSE MUSEUM & ART
GALLERY
ILLUSTRATED ON PAGE 42

POMEGRANATE TEXTILE SAMPLE
DESIGNED IN 1877 BY WILLIAM
MORRIS FOR MORRIS & CO
BLOCK-PRINTED COTTON
TULLIE HOUSE MUSEUM & ART
GALLERY
ILLUSTRATED ON PAGE 37
(DETAIL)

ROSE TEXTILE SAMPLE
DESIGNED IN 1883 BY WILLIAM
MORRIS FOR MORRIS & CO
BLOCK-PRINTED COTTON
TULLIE HOUSE MUSEUM & ART
GALLERY
ILLUSTRATED ON PAGE 32

NEWS FROM NOWHERE
1892
WILLIAM MORRIS
HAMMERSMITH: KELMSCOTT
PRESS
WILLIAM MORRIS SOCIETY

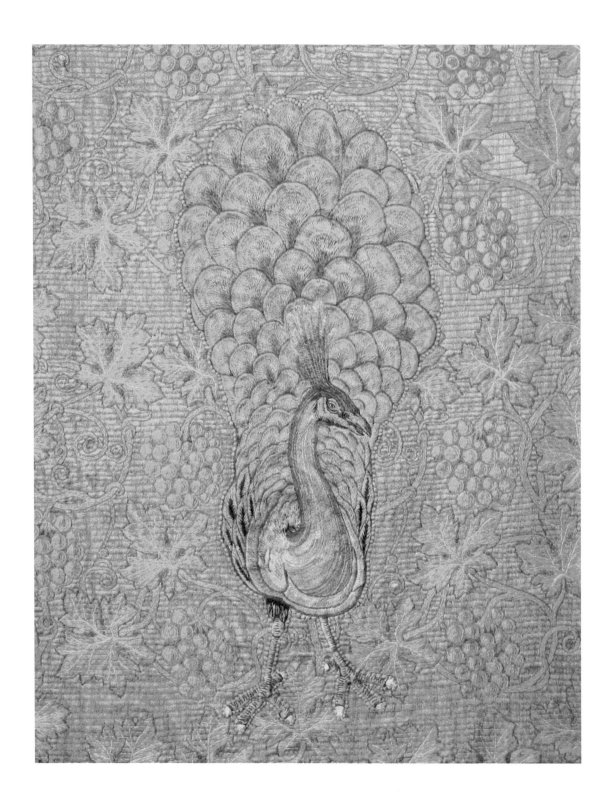

WILLIAM MORRIS
1874
FREDERICK HOLLYER
PHOTOGRAPH
WILLIAM MORRIS SOCIETY

WEY TEXTILE SAMPLE
DESIGNED IN 1883 BY WILLIAM
MORRIS FOR MORRIS & CO
BLOCK-PRINTED COTTON
TULLIE HOUSE MUSEUM & ART
GALLERY
ILLUSTRATED ON PAGE 36

KENNET TEXTILE SAMPLE
DESIGNED IN 1883 BY WILLIAM
MORRIS FOR MORRIS & CO
SILK AND WOOL
TULLIE HOUSE MUSEUM & ART
GALLERY
ILLUSTRATED ON PAGE 35

PEACOCK & DRAGON HANGING
DESIGNED IN 1878 BY WILLIAM
MORRIS FOR MORRIS & CO
JACQUARD WOVEN WOOL
THE COLLECTION OF
STOLBERT ROBINSON
ILLUSTRATED ON PAGE 38
(DETAIL)

PEACOCK & VINE EMBROIDERY
c.1880
DESIGNED BY PHILIP WEBB FOR
MORRIS & CO
WOOL ON LINEN
PRIVATE COLLECTION
ILLUSTRATED ON PAGE 40
(DETAIL)

PLATE
c.1880
DESIGNED BY WILLIAM DE
MORGAN AND DECORATED AT
HIS CHELSEA STUDIO
EARTHENWARE, RUBY LUSTRE
GLAZE
THE COLLECTION OF
STOLBERT ROBINSON

SIGURD THE VOLSUNG
1898
WILLIAM MORRIS
HAMMERSMITH: KELMSCOTT
PRESS
WILLIAM MORRIS GALLERY,
LONDON BOROUGH OF
WALTHAM FOREST

*THE STORY OF GRETTIR THE
STRONG*
1869
TRANSLATED BY
WILLIAM MORRIS &
EIRÍKR MAGNÚSSON
LONDON: FS ELLIS
LAKELAND ARTS TRUST

*FLIGHT OF THE HOLY FAMILY
TO EGYPT* FROM *LIFE OF THE
VIRGIN MARY*
MID-16TH CENTURY
ALBRECHT DURER (1471-1528)
WOODCUT ON PAPER
PRIVATE COLLECTION

THE VISITATION FROM *LIFE OF
THE VIRGIN*
MID-16TH CENTURY
ALBRECHT DURER (1471-1528)
WOODCUT ON PAPER
PRIVATE COLLECTION
ILLUSTRATED ON PAGE 42

SET OF TILES, *THE SEASONS*
EARLY 1860s
DESIGNED BY EDWARD
BURNE-JONES FOR MORRIS,
MARSHALL, FAULKNER & CO
EARTHENWARE
PRIVATE COLLECTION

EXTRACTS FROM CASE FILE
FOR 'YORK CHURCHES –
THREATENED DESTRUCTION'
1884-7
SOCIETY FOR THE PROTECTION
OF ANCIENT BUILDINGS

MANIFESTO OF THE SOCIAL
DEMOCRATIC FEDERATION
1886
WILLIAM MORRIS GALLERY,
LONDON BOROUGH OF
WALTHAM FOREST

STUDIO MAGAZINE, VOL XV
1899
LAKELAND ARTS TRUST
ILLUSTRATED ON PAGE 43

BROTHER RABBIT TEXTILE
SAMPLE
DESIGNED IN 1882 BY WILLIAM
MORRIS FOR MORRIS & CO
BLOCK-PRINTED COTTON
EMERY WALKER TRUST

LOVE IS ENOUGH
1897
WILLIAM MORRIS
ILLUSTRATIONS BY EDWARD
BURNE-JONES
HAMMERSMITH: KELMSCOTT
PRESS
WILLIAM MORRIS SOCIETY

UNDER AN ELM-TREE,
OR THOUGHTS IN THE
COUNTRY-SIDE
1891
WILLIAM MORRIS
LONDON: JAMES LEATHAM
WILLIAM MORRIS SOCIETY

THE NATURE OF GOTHIC
1892
JOHN RUSKIN
HAMMERSMITH: KELMSCOTT
PRESS
WILLIAM MORRIS SOCIETY

THE MANIFESTO OF THE
SOCIALIST LEAGUE
1885
LONDON: SOCIALIST LEAGUE
OFFICE
WILLIAM MORRIS SOCIETY

HOW I BECAME A SOCIALIST
1896
WILLIAM MORRIS
LONDON: THE TWENTIETH
CENTURY PRESS LTD
WILLIAM MORRIS SOCIETY

USEFUL WORK VERSUS USELESS
TOIL
1893
WILLIAM MORRIS
LONDON: WREEVES
WILLIAM MORRIS SOCIETY

A DREAM OF JOHN BALL
1888
WILLIAM MORRIS
LONDON: REEVES & TURNER
WILLIAM MORRIS SOCIETY

CHANTS FOR SOCIALISTS
1892
WILLIAM MORRIS
LONDON: SOCIALIST LEAGUE
OFFICE
WILLIAM MORRIS SOCIETY

ART & SOCIALISM
1884
WILLIAM MORRIS
LEEK BIJOU REPRINTS, NO VII
WILLIAM MORRIS SOCIETY

THE WOOD BEYOND THE WORLD
1894
WILLIAM MORRIS
HAMMERSMITH: KELMSCOTT
PRESS
WILLIAM MORRIS SOCIETY

THE STORY OF THE GLITTERING
PLAIN
1894
WILLIAM MORRIS
ILLUSTRATIONS BY WALTER
CRANE
HAMMERSMITH: KELMSCOTT
PRESS
WILLIAM MORRIS SOCIETY

SOCIALIST LEAGUE
(HAMMERSMITH BRANCH)
MEMBERSHIP CARD
1889
WILLIAM MORRIS SOCIETY

TYPOGRAPHICAL AND BORDER
SAMPLES & DESIGNS
1890-96
BY WILLIAM MORRIS FOR THE
KELMSCOTT PRESS
PENCIL AND INK ON PAPER
WILLIAM MORRIS SOCIETY

DRINKING GLASSES OWNED BY
GEORGE HOWARD
c.1895
DESIGNED BY HARRY POWELL
AND MANUFACTURED BY
JAMES POWELL & SONS,
WHITEFRIARS
THE COUNTRY SEAT

BOUND VOLUME
OF PHOTOGRAPHIC
ENLARGEMENTS OF 15TH
CENTURY PRINTING TYPES
MADE BY EMERY WALKER,
PRESENTED BY WILLIAM
MORRIS TO HIS TYPEFOUNDER
TALBOT BAINES REED, 1891
ST BRIDE PRINTING LIBRARY

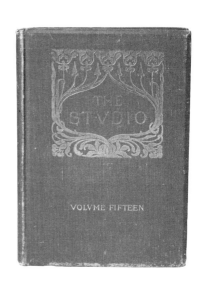

WILLIAM MORRIS
A TRAIL THROUGH
ENGLAND'S NORTH WEST

There could be no better place than the North West to explore the time in which William Morris lived, nor his exceptional legacy. Morris advocated an abandonment of capitalism at a time when the Industrial Revolution had made Britain, and especially the North West, the 'Workshop of the World', the 'Powerhouse of Britain'. It was here where the realities of mass-production were evident in mills and factories as big and powerful as anywhere in Europe. It was also in the North West where reformers and radical movements gave birth to new ideas that aimed to improve the lot of the working person, from Socialism to the Co-operative Movement.

Morris spent time in the North West for artistic and political purposes. His affection for parts of Cumberland and Westmorland is touched upon in this catalogue. Between 1875 and 1878 he spent much time in Leek near Macclesfield, lodging with Thomas and Elizabeth Wardle. The Wardle's Leek-based firm was renowned for dyeing textiles and Morris immersed himself in learning the complexities of the process ("taking in dyeing at every pore", he said). In 1883 Morris & Co. set up a shop in Manchester, aiming to attract customers from the artistic middle classes. Throughout the 1880s Morris spoke on Socialism to large audiences in Liverpool, Preston, Lancaster and Manchester.

Industrial Powerhouse celebrates the rich industrial heritage of England's Northwest. We have included a brief 'trail' around the North West of venues that represent the rapidly changing era in which Morris lived, as well as his life's work and legacy. We hope it will inspire visits to some of the North West's most unique and fascinating attractions.

CHESHIRE

The Macclesfield School of Art & Science opened in 1879 to train designers for work in the silk industry; by the turn of the century it was one of the leading art schools in the country. The School is now **Park Lane Galleries**, part of the **Macclesfield Silk Museum**, and tells the story of how designers and weavers were trained for work in the silk industry.

Nearby **Paradise Mill** contains 26 restored jacquard hand-looms with guides demonstrating the intricate process of weaving. Macclesfield was a centre for silk production and Morris used the Macclesfield firm Brough, Nicholson & Co. for silk weaving even when he had his own looms set up. Morris set out to understand the complexities of silk weaving, hiring a weaver from France with specific skills and later recruiting unemployed weavers from Spitalfields who had lost their jobs in the declining London silk trade. **www.macclesfield.silk.museum**

Englesea Brook Chapel, near Crewe, tells the story of how the working class religious movements of the 19th century brought ordinary people together for prayer, hymns and preaching. The Museum explores the origins of Primitive Methodism, a movement inspired by the American idea of open air camp meetings. Many ordinary people took on roles as local preachers and Sunday School teachers within Methodism and some used the skills and ideas they developed in chapel to become prominent trade union leaders and Liberal politicians. In its very early days Primitive Methodism provided a space in which women could defy the boundaries of gender to become preachers. Morris's philosophies echoed much of the radical social agenda of Methodism though he may have balked at the temperance emphasis of some Primitive Methodists or a bizarre early controversy that led to a temporary ban on preachers wearing trousers. **www.engleseabrook-museum.org.uk**

TOP: LEEK EMBROIDERY 'KIT' SHOWING A DETAIL OF WILLIAM MORRIS'S *INDIAN POPPY* DESIGN, MACCLESFIELD SILK MUSEUM

MIDDLE: HANDLOOMS AT PARADISE MILL MACCLESFIELD SILK MUSEUM

BOTTOM: ENGLESEA BROOK CHAPEL

TOP: FARFIELD MILL

BOTTOM: STAINED GLASS AT THE PEOPLE'S
HISTORY MUSEUM

CUMBRIA

Blackwell, The Arts & Crafts House in Bowness-on-Windermere, is considered the finest surviving example in the UK of the work of its architect, MH Baillie-Scott (1865-1945). Baillie-Scott was one of the key members of the 'second generation' of Arts & Crafts designers, heavily influenced by William Morris. Blackwell's decoration is rich with botanical motifs, local materials, traditional handicraft and salvaged architectural details, as advocated by Morris, and is furnished with works by Baillie Scott, William de Morgan and other designers of the era. **www.blackwell.org.uk**

Farfield Mill is a vibrant arts and heritage centre housed in a converted Victorian woollen mill. Displays show the mill from Victorian heyday and 1950s decline to its restoration and subsequent re-launch as a visitor attraction. Working Dobcross looms weave woollen cloth, and displays explore local cottage industries such as the 'Terrible Knitters of Dent' and sheep farming. The Mill provides workshops where craftspeople make and sell goods, demonstrating the continuation of the craft skills that William Morris sought to foster. **www.farfieldmill.org**

GREATER MANCHESTER

The People's History Museum in Manchester explores many of the world-changing ideas fought for by the working people of Britain, and charts the history of democracy from the early 18th century to the present. In 2010 the museum re-opened after a multi-million pound redevelopment, which sees the museum in a newly extended flagship building. The museum provides a journey through the lives, histories and issues of the working people of Britain, and houses an unprecedented collection of almost 1,500 historic objects, including a photograph of Morris at a Socialist League meeting and Morris-inspired artworks. **www.phm.org.uk**

Salford's **Working Class Movement Library** records over 200 years of organising and campaigning by ordinary men and women. The collection provides a rich insight into working people's daily lives and the roles they played in the significant events of their time. Amassed by Edmund and Ruth Frow, the collection includes books, pamphlets, photographs, songs and archives, incorporating some of the earliest trade union documents in existence. Also in the collections are political songs by William Morris, including 'A Death Song' written for the funeral of a protester killed during a political demonstration, Morris pamphlets such as *A Factory as it Might Be* and *Useful Work Versus Useless Toil*, as well as a Kelmscott Press edition *News from Nowhere*. **www.wcml.org.uk**

LANCASHIRE

Blackburn Museum & Art Gallery houses the collection of Robert Edward Hart (1876-1946), who bequeathed his outstanding collection of numismatics, books and manuscripts to the town. Highlights include illuminated manuscripts from the mid 13th to early 16th century, a leaf from the Gutenberg Bible, early copies of Shakespeare's plays, an edition of Morris's masterpiece *Kelmscott Chaucer* and a Kelmscott edition of *The Well at the World's End*. The building itself reflects the Arts & Crafts style as well as the Gothic revival and was opened as a public museum and library in 1874. **www.blackburn.gov.uk/museums**

The **Rochdale Pioneers Museum** celebrates the success of the Rochdale Equitable Pioneers' Society which is widely regarded as being the first successful retail Co-operative society. The Museum is housed in the original building where the Pioneers opened their doors for business for the first time in 1844 with £28 in capital raised from their 28 members. The Pioneers' 'Model of Consumer co-operation' has now grown into a global movement with 800 million members in 100 countries. William Morris ran Morris & Co. on the co-operative principle and registered the William Morris Co-operative Society in 1893 to provide funds for building a socialist hall in Walthamstow. **museum.co-op.ac.uk**

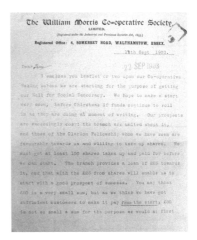

TOP: WORKING CLASS MOVEMENT LIBRARY

MIDDLE: DETAIL AT BLACKBURN ART GALLERY & MUSEUM

BOTTOM: LETTER FROM THE WILLIAM MORRIS CO-OPERATIVE SOCIETY FROM THE NATIONAL CO-OPERATIVE ARCHIVE

TOP: BRIDGE HOUSE AT PORT SUNLIGHT,
ONCE HOME TO WILLIAM LEVER

MIDDLE: LADY LEVER ART GALLERY

BOTTOM: SEFTON PARK PALM HOUSE

LIVERPOOL

William Hesketh Lever (later Viscount Leverhulme) founded **Port Sunlight Village**, built in 1888 for Lever Brothers (now Unilever) factory workers. In the words of the founder it was built "to socialize and Christianize business relations and get back again in the office, factory and workshop to that close family brotherhood that existed in the good old days of hand labour". William Morris advocated that workers should be well cared for and, like Lever at Port Sunlight, created accommodation and allotments at his Merton factory. **www.portsunlight.org.uk**

Nearby the **Lady Lever Art Gallery** contains Lever's huge collection of paintings and sculpture, including many works by Pre-Raphaelites such as Edward Burne-Jones, Dante Gabriel Rossetti and Sir John Everett Millais, who were among Morris's circle. **www.liverpoolmuseums.org.uk/ladylever**

Completed in 1896, **Sefton Park Palm House** was a gift to the City by Henry Yates Thompson. Designed in the tradition of the glass houses by Joseph Paxton, designer of the Crystal Palace, it was stocked with a rich collection of exotic plants. After gradually becoming derelict it was closed in 1980; by 1992 a group was formed to save it and it was restored in 2001. It is now managed as a visitor attraction with a lively events programme and is available for hire for private parties and weddings. Those who campaigned to save the extraordinary building were following in the footsteps of Morris's Society for the Protection of Ancient Buildings which remains a campaigning force for architectural history today. **www.palmhouse.org.uk**

INDUSTRIAL POWERHOUSE

The Industrial Powerhouse website includes information on over 100 fascinating places to visit in the North West with a link to the region's industrial past, as well as a variety of annual events, trails, themed itineraries and guided walks.

Find out more at **www.industrialpowerhouse.co.uk**

Blackwell
The Arts & Crafts House
Bowness-on-Windermere
Cumbria, LA23 3JT
015394 46139
www.blackwell.org.uk

Front & Back Cover:
Design for *Bird* textile
1878
Designed by William Morris for
Morris & Co
Pencil and watercolour
© William Morris Society

William Morris
1874
Frederick Hollyer
Photograph
© William Morris Society

Inside Cover:
Marigold Textile Sample
Designed in 1875 by William Morris
for Morris & Co
Block-printed cotton
© Tullie House Museum & Art Gallery

ACKNOWLEDGEMENTS

Industrial Powerhouse
Inspired by Innovation

Supported by

EUROPEAN REGIONAL DEVELOPMENT FUND

Printed on 'Zen' paper, supplied by
James Cropper Speciality Papers.

MORRIS & C⁰

To visit your nearest Morris & Co.
retailer or request samples visit
www.william-morris.co.uk or
use the contact details below.

London Showroom
Tel: 0844 543 4749
Email: enquiries@a-sanderson.co.uk

Head Office
Tel: 0844 543 9500
Email: enquiries@a-sanderson.co.uk

We would like to express our gratitude to the following, whose
generous assistance made this exhibition and catalogue possible:

The Society of Antiquaries of London
Birmingham Museum and Art Gallery
Blackburn Museum & Art Gallery
The British Museum
National Co-operative Archive & Rochdale Pioneers Museum
The Country Seat
Helen Elletson
The Emery Walker Trust
Englesea Brook Chapel and Museum
Peter Faulkner
The Fitzwilliam Museum
The Golsoncott Foundation
The Honourable Mr Philip Howard
Patrons and Benefactors of the Lakeland Arts Trust
Macclesfield Silk Museum
The People's History Museum
Private Lenders
Paul Reeves
J.S.M. Scott Esq.
Sefton Park Palm House Preservation Trust
Society for the Protection of Ancient Buildings
St Bride Printing Library
Tullie House Museum & Art Gallery
The Whitworth Art Gallery
The William Morris Gallery
The William Morris Society
The Working Class Movement Library